Unbroken Pieces

Unbroken Pieces: A collection of poems by Sharla Fanous

Published by Bella Press
P.O. Box 45010
Kanata, ON K2M 2Y1
Visit the author's website at https://sharlafanous.com

Cover design by Bella Press
Cover and Interior Art by Mariah Seedorf
Proofreading by Book Magic
Formatting for print by Indie Publishing Group
Author Photo by Melanie Mathieu Photography
ISBN: 978-1-7779187-4-3 (paperback)
ISBN: 978-1-7779187-3-6 (hardcover)

First Edition

Dedication

For Erin and Caitlin -
may you continue to be resilient and brave

Contents

Acknowledgements

I want to acknowledge Rachel Marie Kang and Indelible Ink Writers for reminding me of my love for writing poetry and creating a wonderful community to share my art and learn and be inspired.

I also want to acknowledge Mariah Seedorf, who created the graphic art on the cover.

Introduction

Poetry has been a lifeline for me since I was about fifteen years old. Although I never felt safe to express emotions outwardly, my pen could always find the exact words to convey the thoughts that ran through my mind. For a period, I forgot that I possessed this ability. Like many women, I so lost myself in caring for my family that I forgot my own passions. But I have recently rediscovered them and I am thrilled to share them with you, the reader.

This first compilation of poems centers around the themes of reflection and discovery. Reflecting on where I have been and discovering who I am and want to be. I write about identity, family, friendship, love, heartbreak, hope, and faith. My desire is that you can find pieces of yourself in my words as these themes are a part of the collective human experience.

Unbroken Pieces

A Collection of Poems

Sharla Fanous

Inspired

I read the work of a stranger
And it reminded me that words can drip like honey
That phrases can be sweet morsels
Intricately prepared and
Delicately nibbled or voraciously devoured
By lovers of the poetic.

A desire that long lay dormant awakened within me
My pen finding inspiration in everything
In dreams long forgotten,
In hours' long phone calls,
In days long—far, far too long,
In my brokenness and in my wholeness
In my Creator who created me in His image
To create.

Blue Tones

I exist in blue tones,
Reposing peacefully in tranquil cerulean,
Laughing joyfully in playful turquoise,
Sinking sadly into deep, dark midnight,
Drifting pensively in melancholic ocean,
Rising audaciously in bold indigo,
Soft-spoken passion in unassuming violet.
I exist in blue tones.

On the Day I Was Born

Under a waxing, gibbous moon
Just minutes into a new day
I cried for the very first time.
Naked and innocent, a tiny display,
Disco was dying, slowly and sure.
Britain's election denied to a man
Yet on the very day that I was born,
Five were murdered by the Klan.
I came into a world full of hope,
Hope is how my life started,
Yet I entered a world full of hate
And I fear that is how I'll depart it.

She

In defiant beauty
She wears her coils as a crown
Comfortable in her own skin
Tawny and brown
Round nose
Lips full
All that she is—
Beautiful!
Unique and strong
Though relentlessly tried,
Her peace and true beauty
Reside inside.

New England State of Mind

Newly cut grass and autumn leaves
Wood burning and apple trees,
Falling rain and mud-soaked paths
Clean sheets and Ivory soap baths,
Open meadows and mountain springs
Wild flowers and old buildings,
Ocean air and stacks of books
Freshly brewed coffee and hidden nooks,
In these scents, I take comfort wherever I roam.
I close my eyes, breathe in, and for a moment, I am home.

Who Am I?

Who am I?
A daughter of a Black, free-spirited flower child,
A granddaughter of a stern, southern preacher woman,
A great granddaughter to a first-generation freedwoman,
A great-great granddaughter of a slave.
My tree leans far to the left
Hanging low on one side
So that the fruit is easy to reach.
But the other side is so high,
When I try to glance at the fruit,
The sun blinds my eyes.
Who am I?
A daughter of a white man,
A granddaughter of a white man,
A great-granddaughter of a white man,
A great-great granddaughter of a white man,
That is not enough knowledge for me
So I will shake the tree
Until it tells me who I am.

Introvert

Away from everyone and happy.
Able to be alone and daydream,
Make everything the way you want it,
Because it is only in your dreams
That everything is perfect.
I want to be away from everyone and happy,
Lost in my perfect world in my dreams.

A Sister's Love

Baby brother crying,
Mommy sleeping
Too deep to hear him calling.
"It's okay." My voice calming,
My tiny body holding
His tinier body
Laying him gently on the living room floor.
Always observing
Watching and learning
The things that mothers do recalling,
"It's okay." My hands cleaning
And methodically folding
A new diaper in place.
Examining my work critically in the dimly lit room.

The Child

His eyes were as blue as a clear sky
On a summer's day.
His brown, winding curls tumbled over his forehead
And around his pudgy face.
As he sat up,
He stretched his round, plump arms
Toward me.
Small streams of tears stained his reddened cheeks
And flowed to the corners of his small, thin lips.
His tiny fingers stretched out from his dimpled hands
To reach mine.
And when he caught them,
He looked up
And smiled.

Take Me Back

Take me back to the wonder-filled summers of my childhood.
Trying to find the perfect stick to dig for worms,
Not even a hint of wincing as they squirmed in our hands.
Take me back to the wonder-filled summers of my childhood.
The joy of making mud pies,
Lining them up on the porch steps to "cool,"
Pretending the scent of apple,
blueberry, and cherry filled the air.
Take me back to the wonder-filled summers of my childhood.
The sheer exhilaration of rolling down steep grassy hills,
Landing on our backs in a fit of giggles
As we stared at the clear blue sky.
Take me back to the wonder-filled summers of my childhood.
Popping off the heads of dandelions and making flower crowns,
Watching in awe as tiny, black ants carried crumbs on their backs.
Take me back to the wonder-filled summers of my childhood.
At the end of those happy days,
Caked in dirt and sweat,
Soaking in a lukewarm bath
Until fingers wrinkled
And the whites of our nails reappeared.

Brave

Young girl
Crushed by fear
Sits rocking anxiously, covering her ears.
Piercing screams fill the air in response to
The bass tone tremor of thinly veiled threats.

Young girl
Teeming with fright
Flees with quickening steps into the dark night,
Seeking shelter, she makes her way to escape
The horror and the noise.

Young girl,
Proud and poised,
Returns with courage to use her voice
Her life will not be spent fearing the insecurity
At the other end of any man's fists.

Young girl
Full of dreams
Carries her confidence under her wings.
She lifts off with hope as her guide
To a world of her own choosing.

Rescue

A hole
So deep, it seems unfillable.
The dark,
The only witness to her tears and confessions of her longings
for connection.
She feels destined
To be alone,
Unloved,
Undesired,
Unable to feel the freedom of being
Known,
Understood.
Who would love her?
A girl so lost inside herself?
Untrusting,
She built walls for protection,
Yet
It seems that her fortified heart is also her
Prison.
Is there someone who can rescue her from herself,
From the tower built with her own hands,
Locked from the inside?
Who can she trust with the key to unlock this door
When she cannot even trust herself?
Maybe,
Maybe if someone were able to get close enough to
Pry the key clutched tightly in her hands,

They could set her free.
But the door is heavily guarded from the outside
By dragons carrying the memories of
Abandonment and neglect,
Of sinister hags and fallen princes.
These dragons, too, both protect and imprison her.
Maybe,
Maybe I am not worthy of such a fight?
She thinks as she witnesses, time and again,
Knights fall or flee in an attempt to reach her.
This is her fate.
She must accept it,
Yet
It is she who holds the key.
Maybe,
Maybe she should stop waiting to be rescued.
Maybe she could be brave and free herself.
The key
The key she holds in her hand was forged in
The promises of her Father.
"You, my child, are a daughter of the King.
Not meant to be a princess cowering in a tower,
But a warrior
Wielding a powerful sword

To slay the dragons that hold you prisoner.
You are wonderfully made,
Of immeasurable value,
And I am always with you.
Be brave, my daughter.

Do not be afraid.
I love you.
I created you because
I chose you.
I have a purpose for you.
I know you better than you know yourself.
I Am
All that you need.
You are never alone."
Filled
As she remembers her Father's words,
She turns the key,
Opens the door.
And with one brave step,
She is free.

I Would Go

I am not one to wander far from home,
But I often crave the calm and quiet places
Instead of the usual cacophony and crowded spaces.
I imagine what it would be like to
Wake up in a countryside
On a crisp, cool morning.
Green, rolling hills still covered in dew,
Long dirt roads lined with large oak trees.
Walking through untouched meadows,
Lying in fields, taking in the fragrances of wildflowers,
Sitting on an old porch swing, listening to the falling rain,
With only the characters in my favourite books for company.
Yes, that is a place I long to be.

Ode to Coffee

A kiss on the lips from you
Wakes me from my slumber
Makes my eyes bright,
Shakes me to life.

I want to drink you in,
Embrace all your warmth.
My face meeting yours, smooth like silk
Chase every single drop.

Even the scent of you
Wills me to move my tired limbs,
Stills the whirring world for a moment,
Fills me with courage to face the day.

Promise to always greet me in the morning
In the silence when nothing else stirs
In the violence of the chaos of hurry
When propensed to long days and short nights.

The Sound of Rain

Like an unceasing "Shh"
As if the heavens are coaxing the earth into silence.
Or a "tap-tap-tap" against the window
Begging you to share your thoughts.
At times, a kind of "plip-plop" slow drip
Tiptoeing on your nose
Or making no sound at all
Placidly misting the air.

My Skin

Like beach sand from the northern coast
Maybe, almond butter on toast
But when the sun kisses my melanin,
It resembles golden caramel or cinnamon.

Lost Year

Spend Easter with my family,
Thanksgiving with my friends,
Girls' trip or solo vacation,
Before the world ends.
Knock some things off the bucket list,
Get a new tattoo,
Explore the city and surroundings,
Go on a date or two.
Send my kids to summer camp,
Or at least send them to school,
Visit Grandma and the aunties,
Spend time at the beach or the pool.
Sip coffee with my colleagues,
Give friends a hug or high-five,
But thanks to the dreaded Corona,
All I managed to do was survive.

So maybe that's not entirely true....

The past year may not have gone
The way that I had planned.
There may have been no road trips
Or a summer in the sand,
But what I gained was time
To be introspective, to be free,
To take some important steps
In rediscovering me.

Before the virus, life moved too fast.
I didn't have time to notice
That inside me lived an artist.
There was a writer, a poetess.
So thank you, 2020
And, yes, Covid-19.
You made the whole world stand still
But you helped me discover my dream.

Lazy Days

Tired and yawning,
It's a good day for a nap
Into sheets I fall.

Unwelcome

He's here again
A most unwelcome guest
He never calls first,
Knocks, or makes a request
To visit.
He just enters unexpected,
My personal space disrespected.
I never know how long he'll stay.
It could be hours, or maybe days.
He sits too close and whispers to me,
Sharp, stabbing words:
"You'll never have that, it will never be
For you."
His lies sound true.
I cry in protest, and I begin to cower,
But he knows no empathy and his voice gets louder.
"No love, no hope,
no time." I can't cope!
Maybe I'll just sleep until he is gone.
There's some relief in disappearing,
But for how long?
I never know how long he'll stay.
It could be hours, or maybe days.

Olivia Grace

Good-bye, little love.
Our hearts once made melody as they beat together,
A happy little tune.
Then one day
Only the off-beat tempo of my own as yours fell silent.
Good-bye, little love.
You held onto me so tight as you made your way to heaven.
'Come with me,' you sang.
Oh, how I want to be with you,
But not yet, little love.
Take Jesus' hand, and He will hold you
Until I come home to you.

My First Place

On a quiet Florida street
Sat a tiny two-bedroom suite.
The kitchen was too small to eat in,
So in the living room, we enjoyed our din.
There was air conditioning, but no heat.
Furniture was bought second-hand or free.
The VCR played "Ten Things.." on repeat,
Because we had no cable TV.
Our washing machine was always broken.
We had a crab grass lawn that we couldn't mow.
In the small bath, the shower ran cold,
And I suspect that there was mould.
It didn't matter, in any case,
For I'll forever cherish my first place.

You Say

I'm too quiet, you say,
My head always in the clouds,
Yet when I speak my truth,
I speak it way too loud.

I'm too different, you say,
My hair is kinky and my eyes are bright.
My skin is too dark for some,
But for others, it's too light.

I'm too good, you say,
I need to loosen up.
I'm too good, yet for you,
I'm not quite good enough.

I'm too broken, you say,
I'll never love quite right,
Yet it's love that binds my broken pieces,
And holds them together tight.

Fear of Crashing

Trying not to think
Of plunging to certain death,
Hands gripping tightly.

Home

How can time stand still
Yet always run out?
Unlike our words and stories,
There's always more to say.
With you, it's all truth and trust,
Comfort and calm,
Safety and ease.
You feel like home,
And I never want to leave.

Make You Feel My Love

I can see the pain behind your eyes
Though you try so hard to disguise it,
But it's hard, so hard, to hide your hurt
From one who can so easily recognize it.
Others may not notice the damage,
The wound may be difficult for them to see.
To me it is so obvious,
Because the same was once in me.
If I hold you long and close,
As tightly as a glove,
Could I help you see your worth?
Could I make you feel my love?

I wish I could repair all that's broken,
Put you together piece by piece.
I would take it all on me,
If it meant your pain would cease.
I would make space for you,
Leave room for you to speak.
I would be a safe place for you
When you're feeling weary and weak.
So let me hold you long and close,
Wrap you tightly as a glove,
Let me help you see your worth,
Make you feel my love.

I Want to Know You

I want to know you
Not who you pretend to be.
The soul behind the mask
Is who I long to see.
I want to know what moves you,
What inspires your curiosity.
I want to know your past
What has caused your heart to bleed.
I want to know the thoughts
That hide behind those eyes.
I want to know why you smile.
When will you drop the disguise?
I know there is more to you
Than who you pretend to be.
Won't you let me behind the curtain?
I promise you're safe with me.

Get Up!

I watch her as she lies there restlessly,
Curled up fetally, face wincing.
Get up, girl!
It did not break you,
Only bent you in unimaginable ways.
Get up, girl!
It's time to untangle yourself
And stretch your limbs.
You'll find that the bending changed you.
You can reach higher
Persevere longer.
Get up, girl!
Life still goes on around you,
There's still more for you to live,
More love, more laugher,
More hope, more discovery.
Get up, girl!
t's time to rise above what was,
Stand in what is,
And walk toward what will be.
Slowly, uncurling, she sits up,
Dizzy from retiring so long.
She shifts her body and plants her feet,
Still unsure if her legs can bear
The weight of the pain she carries.
I give her an assuring nod.
Get up, girl!

She breathes in long and deep
And rises to find that
She is stronger and somehow taller than before.
Her wincing face relaxes, then tightens.
But it's not pain anymore.
It's determination.
Yes, girl, like that!

Here

If there is any place that I should be able to call home,
It is here.
The same blood may not flow through our veins,
But the same blood covers our shame.
Therefore, we are family here.
But why does my brother ignore me?
And why does my sister reject me?
Are the things that are different between us
Really stronger than the thing that is the same?
Love is supposed to live here.
Acceptance I should find here.
But I don't and my faith is shaken
And I don't want to stay here,
Because what I have believed
Is not what I have experienced,
And I don't know where to go from here.

These Days

These days when the silence is loud, the crowds lonely,
and sleep restless,
When thoughts smother, limbs languish, and feelings betray,
When nothing brings comfort because everything seems heavy.
These days when the mind doesn't want to think, body move,
or heart feel,
When the weariness overwhelms, the longing despairs,
the hurriedness exhausts,
When something has to give because everything seems to take.
These days God says to me, "Listen for My voice,
seek My presence, abide with Me.
"Come to Me, and I will speak to you,
I will strengthen you, I will hold you.
Come to Me, and I will carry you and make everything light."
These days God says to me, "Let your mind rest,
your body still, your heart be fallow.
"Come to Me, and I will unburden you,
I will restore you, I will renew you.
Come to Me, and I will give you abundantly
more than what anything can take."

Comfort

The Lord found me
Lost in a desert place,
Dry from all my weeping,
Faint from the pain.
"Take my hand, My daughter."
He held it firmly, for I was weak.
He led me through a narrow path.
I followed Him closely,
My steps matching His.
He told me things that
I had forgotten:
About where I had been,
Where I was going,
And to Whom I belonged.
With each word
And each step with the Word,
I felt strength returning.
He never left me.
We journeyed together,
My hand in His
Until I felt whole again.
"Go and do likewise," he said.
As I was walking along,
I saw a young woman,
Lost in a desert place,
Dry from all her weeping,
Faint from the pain.
"Take my hand, my sister.
I know the way."

It Is Finished

"It is finished."
I heard You cry Your last
After You cried for thirst.
I remember holding You in my arms,
When You cried Your first.
I witnessed as they came to worship.
I listened as they bowed and praised.
Lowly shepherds and wealthy kings,
I wondered and stood amazed.
I listened as they sang, "Hosanna!"
And laid palms down at Your feet.
In horror, I witnessed, as the same
Cried out, "Crucify Him, crucify Him!" on repeat.
I watched You grow in wisdom.
I observed You with pride.
My son, yet the Son of God,
I watched You as You died.
It is finished, it is over.
I know You were never mine to have.
I was merely a vessel to carry You
Into the world You came to save.
"It is finished."
How can it be over,
When we've just begun?
We followed You for three years
And now it is done?
We watched as You healed

The sick, the blind, the possessed.
We witnessed as You loved
The poor, the outcast, the oppressed.
You fed five thousand men.
You raised the dead to life.
You calmed stormy waters.
You were peace amid the strife.
You were our teacher,
Our counsellor and our friend.
We were unworthy and uneducated,
Yet You made us "fishers of men."
It is finished, it is over.
Where do we go from here?
Without our leader, without our Messiah,
We are scattered and live in fear.
"It is finished."
Father, my mission is complete.
I have saved all that were lost.
Their debt is fully paid
With my blood on this cross.
Father, forgive them.
They know not what they've done.
When they drove in these nails,
They hung their Creator, God's Son.
They may not see it now,
But soon they will understand.
That I willingly laid my life down.
It was all part of the Master's plan.
Let my blood satisfy Your justice.
Let my love satisfy Your law.

Erase every sin.
Cover every flaw.
It is finished; it is over.
Mission accomplished; job is done.
Into Thy hands, I commit My Spirit.
Oh Father, receive Your Son!
"It is finished."
Your cry was victorious!
For death and sin You defeated.
All sins are forgiven.
At the Father's right hand, You are seated.
You died and bore the full weight of my sin.
For me, You suffered scorn and humiliation.
You were bruised and You were battered
To rescue me from my depravation.
Before You spoke the world into existence,
Before the first day of Creation,
You knew the world would need a Saviour.
Your death was planned before the foundation.
Your love is incomprehensible.
It is beyond human understanding.
You, Son of God, died for me.
You, Prince of Heaven, with angels commanding.
It is finished, but it's not over.
It has only just begun,
Because I serve a risen Saviour.
Your work in me is not yet done.

You See Me

You see me,
The real me,
The broken and the unhealed me,
The "one who is afraid to fail" me.
You see me.
I can't conceal me,
The insecurities that reveal me,
The "I don't want to feel" me.
You see me.
You hear me,
The quiet inside of me,
The thoughts that terrify in me,
The tears that I refuse to cry in me.
You hear me,
The dreams that hide in me,
Even the ones that have died in me,
The "I don't even want to try" in me.
You hear me.
You love me,
Every single part of me,
The soul and the heart of me,
Your masterpiece, the art of me.
You love me.
You are a part of me,
The end and the start of me,
The very beating heart of me.
You love me.
How incomprehensible it is to be fully known
And still fully loved by You.

For the Broken

Torn away and torn apart,
Too young to remember,
Too young to understand,
But not too young to be
Broken.
Alone and often out of place,
A longing to belong,
Feeling the weight of loneliness,
Would I always be this
Broken?
Even love didn't last,
Leaving shattered pieces,
Shards of glass.
I guess I was always meant to be
Broken.
But God collected all the pieces of me,
Traced the fractured seams with His fingers,
Filled in the spaces with His love and grace,
Making this vessel whole again.
A perfect masterpiece
For His love to pour in,
His love to pour out
To the Broken.

Choose Joy

For too long you've been afraid
To experience the fullness of joy,
Thinking that if you held it so precious,
And felt it so complete,
The loss of it would destroy you.
How foolish to hold onto the belief
That you cannot lose what you do not have.
Why choose to live in the fear of loss
When you can choose joy?
It's like deciding to live in a world of grey
For fear of loving colour too much.
You can't avoid pain by dismissing joy.
Pain will always come,
But so will joy if you let it in.
So choose joy!
In all of its complete wonder
Let its warmth fill you
And you'll find that joy is the best remedy for the pain.

Part of Me

LORD, help me to understand
That seeing is not believing
That my feelings are not facts
Because there is a part of me that is
Flooded with hopelessness in impossible situations.
There is a part of me that is
Fearful that loneliness is a permanent state.
There is a part of me that is
Worried that there is not enough.
There is a part of me that is
Confused about what to do next.
There is a part of me that is
Overwhelmed by what I think I cannot do.
There is a part of me that is
Overcome by the grief of losses.
There is a part of me that is
Unsettled by all the chaos in the world.
LORD, let there be a greater part of me
Whose faith is not sight
ut knows the God who is "I Am."
In hopelessness, You say, "I Am Faithful."
In loneliness, You say, "I Am Present."
In scarcity, You say, "I Am your Provider."
In confusion, You say, "I Am the Way"
In inadequacy, You say, "I Am your Help."
In grief, You say, "I Am your Comforter."
In chaos, You say, "I Am your Sustainer."

LORD, I know that You hold the whole world in Your hands.
Help me to know that even I am held securely by You
Because there is a part of me that needs reminding.
There is a part of me that needs to hear You speak
In a still small voice, letting me know that I am never alone.

Dance It Out

When life gets heavy
The stress is steady
My body holds all the tensions in
Muscles stiff, emotions pressing from within
Aching to get out
Pressure building
My body longing
For relief.
When peace is too brief
Girl, it's time to dance it out!
Sometimes, all it takes
Is a gentle sway
To some slow, bluesy sound.
At other times, that is too mild
And I need to move free and wild
Completely unbound,
Limbs shifting rhythmically
Feeling the beauty of sweet release.
Sometimes, you just need to
Dance it out!
Safe
When the boat rocked
And the storm raged
And the strong winds began to blow,
I placed my trust in the Saviour who made me
To never let me go.
The boat still rocks

The storm still rages
The strong winds still blow and blow,
But in the palm of His hand,
My Father still holds me,
And He will never let me go.

Rain

It's coming on,
Like clouds that gather and darken before a storm,
And I cannot stop it.
I can feel it building,
Covering every part of me,
From the inside out,
In this empty solitude,
I feel so alone.
Even if I were to scream,
No one would hear me crying,
Or see that I am drowning in my tears.
Yet, just when I think
The darkness has overtaken me,
That the flood has swallowed me up,
The sun breaks through the clouds,
Drying up my sorrow,
And covering me in warm light
Once again.

I Didn't Want to Go

I didn't want to go.
You didn't interest me
Beyond the fact that
You were interesting.
Curious about your craft,
Impressed by the studied way
You set about your goals.
I did indeed find you fascinating.
But when you asked me out,
I didn't want to go.

The thought of first impressions,
Agonizing over what to wear
And what to do with my hair,
Which didn't much cooperate
In this summer humidity.
Would it be anything but frustrating?
I was through with dating.
It was all but disappointing.
So, I didn't want to go.

"Go and have fun," my friends urged.
More versed and experienced than I
In the world of men and courtship.
"What's the worst that could happen?"
They argued points seemingly valid.
I could have a terrible time

And we would never speak again.
I guess that wouldn't be the end of the world.
Still, I didn't want to go.

But, out of excuses, I went.
And you quickly calmed me with your smile.
You took me on a tour of our city.
We talked for hours of the past, the present, and the hopeful future.
We sat closer, stood closer, moved closer.
Like magnets unable to resist the pull.
And when the night was over,
I didn't want to go.

Charades

You're mine and I'm yours.
At least that is what they say.
People even envy us.
They wish they could have what we do.
It's funny what people see when they're
On the outside looking in.
Why would it be obvious to them,
There is no us, no you and me?
Maybe it's how we look at each other,
Like we have a secret that we won't share.
Or maybe it's how we seem to be inseparable,
Always together— the cute perfect couple.
Everyone suspects, they all assume.
Best friends, family, even I'm a fool.
But this game that we're playing
Isn't fun anymore.
Because it is just a game—to you.
I can't allow my heart to be played with.
I'm not an object for your amusement,
Or for the audience that has gathered around us.
I'm sorry.
I was never very good at charades.

Insomnia

You have taken away my sleep.
You have stolen it, along with my heart,
Leaving me only with thoughts of you.
Could it be that I'm falling for you?
Yeah, so hard that it hurts,
For there is nothing to break it.
Could you be the one?
Unexpected, Undeniable.
But I shouldn't, I can't, I won't
Let you.
You're not what I expected love to be.
You're not my fantasy, my ideal, my prince.
But you're reality, real—
Which is more than a dream come true.
The way you look at me,
The way you make me smile.
How could I live without that?
You have reached a part of me
No one could touch
And
You have taken away my sleep.

Rainbows

Sometimes, I catch myself smiling
When I'm thinking of you.
It's like sunshine through crystal,
Making a rainbow on the wall
And anyone who sees it stands in awe.
You are that sunshine,
and my smiles are rainbows.
Like the light that bends and breaks through crystal
To form a colourful masterpiece
For all to admire.
So, thoughts of you flow through me
Creating a beautiful glow on my face.
It always surprises me,
And I have to laugh,
Knowing that if anyone were watching,
They would stop and stare,
As if to study a rainbow on a wall.

I Don't Want to Miss You

My mind races toward you
Like it's searching for a place to rest.
My heart aches for you.
Does the same pain rise in your chest?
I'm trying so hard to say good-bye.
To let go, to move on,
But I keep coming back to missing you.
Are we really over? Are you gone?
That one dimple in your cheek
When you smile,
The glint in your hazel eyes
When you tease,
That high-tone laugh
When you're really amused.
I don't want to miss all of these.
We can't miss this moment.
I think we should try.
There should be an "us."
Don't let this be good-bye.
Am I crazy?
Is this all in my head?
You wanted me too.
Isn't that what you said?
We have lightning in a bottle.
Our connection can't compare.
If what we have is magic,
Can we make it reappear?

Are we really going to mess this up?
Let it slip through our hands?
Shouldn't we fight for this?
Can't let us be over before we begin.

Stranger Danger

There was something odd about you,
Strange and getting stranger.
But like an insect to the light blue,
I was attracted to the danger.
Flashing lights and sounding alarms
Did not manage to scare me.
Instead I wandered toward your arms,
As if someone had dared me.
Ignoring warnings, disregarding signs,
I was on a mission to uncover the good,
But you're not the good kind.
I just thought you were misunderstood.
Now I'm caught in your trap,
Just a fly in your web.
I cannot escape,
My misstep, my regret.

The Performance

I thought my search was over,
I thought I'd found the one
Who checked all the boxes,
The elusive unicorn.
You knew exactly what to say,
The words dripped like dew from your lips.
You drew me in with your beautiful mind,
Your tender heart and your quips.
You sang me a song and put on a show,
But your magic was just an illusion.
You cast your spell, you played your tricks,
Then left me alone in confusion.
Your frame so unassuming, your voice so sweet,
So many kisses you'd stolen
Until I realized much too late
You're just a wolf in sheep's clothing.

Let Love Decide

We said it from the start,
That we didn't make sense.
We were worlds apart,
Said, "Let's just be friends."
Soon it seemed that my heart
Would be straddling a fence.
Thought we were so smart,
But these feelings grew intense.
I tried so much to resist you,
It would be too complicated.
I knew as soon as I kissed you,
Be it love or our doom, we were fated.
I could not so easily dismiss you,
Your charms were so underrated.
Oh, how badly I missed you!
A place in my heart you created.
Every touch from you was electric,
Being with you was so confusing.
My heart, I tried so hard to protect it,
That battle I was quickly losing.
To be together, I was sceptic,
It seemed all too amusing.
But your love was so magnetic,
And then it was you I was choosing.
I didn't know I was in love with you
Until I had to let you go.
Too many things reminded me of you,

Like every love song on the radio.
How do I think I can find someone new?
Can find anyone else who would know,
How to make me feel safe like you do,
When you hold me close and don't let me go,
I want to hear you say that we're not done,
Though it seems an impossible future awaits
It feels like we have only just begun
The start of something truly great.
Though I fought, my heart you have won,
Honestly, from the very first date.
Come, let's chase the sun,
And leave love to decide our fate.

My Fragile Heart

When I gave you my fragile heart to hold,
When I placed it in your hands,
A thousand times I did withhold.
A thousand doubts I did withstand.
When I gave you my fragile heart to hold,
When I allowed myself to be open,
I breathed a moment carefree and bold,
A moment to have a love to hope in.
When I gave you my fragile heart to hold,
When finally my trust I surrendered,
I didn't know how quickly you'd grow cold.
Learned too late that you weren't a contender.
When I gave you my fragile heart to hold,
When you observed it worn and cracked,
Why pretend and leave the truth untold?
Why not just hand it back?
When I gave you my fragile heart to hold,
When you let it slip from your hands,
A thousand pieces I did behold.
A thousand shards that did land.
Now I have no heart to give,
Now I am as empty as your hands.
Never my heart shall again live.
Never love will it again demand.

One Day

One day, the sound of your name
Won't gnaw at my chest, taking the breath out of my lungs,
Or cause me to face another night of tear-stained pillows.
One day, I'll be able to inhale the scent of sweet summer grass
Without the memory of the taste of our first kiss,
your eyes locked on mine,
The world around us disappearing into a blurry haze
of sunshine.
One day, I'll forget the feeling of your arms around me,
Of being so close to you, yet longing to be closer still,
When the days didn't hold enough hours being held by you.
One day, I won't remember that you broke my heart,
That I was both too much for you, and still not enough.
One moment engulfed by your love,
and the next pushed outside of it.
One day, the memories won't haunt me,
And the ghost of us will disappear.
I just wish it wasn't so hard for me to forget.
Or that it wasn't so easy for you.

Will I Know Love?

If love meets me, will I recognize it?
Will I welcome love or jeopardize it?
I have not seen love to memorize it.
How do I know it's love? Who verifies it?
Men don't seem to want to give or take love.
But only seem to want to "make love."
So they try to offer me a fake love.
But I'm waiting on a higher stakes' love.
My father didn't even know he made me.
The man who vowed to love me betrayed me.
I wish that this didn't jade me.
Are there good ones out there? Persuade me.
Should I wait for one highly regarded,
Who will give his love wholehearted?
Until then, I'll keep my heart closely guarded,
So that I will not be outsmarted.
I decided no longer to look for love.
After all the things I mistook for love,
Or often felt overlooked in love.
So I leave it in the Hands that wrote the Book on love.

Hard Place

I wasn't expecting you to be
All that you were to me.
All anxiety and delight,
My first "good morning,"
My last "good night,"
All of the spaces in between.
You made me feel seen,
Beautiful, wanted,
Cynical, haunted.
We were not the same kind,
So I did not expect to find
Smiles and wishes, dreams and fears,
Whispers and glimpses, heartbreak and tears.
We were a fire burning hot,
Without a care or a thought.
That we weren't meant to last.
It ended so fast.
Although we were worlds apart,
For a brief moment, you held my heart.
I wish I could give you what you wanted,
Be what you needed and more.
But then I wouldn't be the girl,
You would give yourself up for.

Make It Stop

I can't make it stop,
Any of it,
The pain
The tears
The days, weeks, and months going by without you.

I want it to go away,
All of it,
Missing you,
Loving you,
Imagining what it would've been like if you stayed.

I need it back,
At least some of it,
My heart
My mind
The sleep I lose every night thinking of you.

I want you back,
But all or none of you,
Your safety
Your love
Your hands to hold me and make this ache go away.

Things I'll Never Tell You

I'll never tell you that I still believe
It should be you and me.
I'm waiting for you to make your case.

I'll never say that I'm trying so much
To forget your touch,
Or just how much I miss your face.

I'll never tell you that I still cry.
I still question why.
What made you think you couldn't love me?

I'll never tell you that it's not her
You want, no, not her.
That I could give you what you need.

I'll never mention that though I smile,
All the while,
My heart is in a million pieces inside.

I'll never share how everything you said
Plays over and over in my head,
And I wonder if they were just lies.

I'll never tell you and you'll never know.
I love you.
I love you, but I'm letting you go.

What Happens?

I used to believe that broken
Meant that I did not know how to love.
What happens to girls who have not been
Held close, kept safe, or seen?
Was it that I was hiding from love?
Or was it hiding from me?
But it's not that I don't know how to love.
I keep my affections close until I feel safe enough.
Then I love hard and strong and deep.
I can love, but I have found
I can't recognize when someone loves me.
Is it love or deception?
I am often a fool in love
Unable to discern the truth and intentions
Behind the sweet little lies.
What happens to girls who have not been
Held close, kept safe, or seen?
They could fall for anything.

Again

I was convinced that you would hold my heart forever.
That I would never breathe the same again.
You would always imprison my mind,
Whenever I would hear your name again.
I thought replacing you would be futile,
My heart never to be set aflame again.

But here I am lost in easy conversation,
Sharing laughs and making plans again.
Singularly captivating another's attention,
Holding someone's hands again.
Alive with eager anticipation,
Watching two hearts expand again.

I'm no longer waiting for you
To realize what you've lost.
Now I know someone will treasure
What another carelessly tossed.

My heart is breaking free from you.
My lungs breathe in deep again.
Memories of us are quickly fading.
Soundly I can sleep again.
Moving forward and moving on.
I am ready to dive deep again.

Her Story

Once she was a helpless waif,
A child without a voice.
God alone kept her safe,
When too small to make her choices
Heard,
Her Words,
Too soft, too few, too weak,
When she dared to speak.
Yet her cries
Rose high enough
To reach the ears of her Father.
And angels He did send
To defend,
Her wounds tend.
He, Himself, did bend
To mend
Her brokenness.

Once she was a lonely girl,
A misfit who befriended books.
Seemed out of place in the real world,
Peculiar in her manner, and her looks
Absurd
A rare bird,
All limbs, and eyes, and hair
But she grew fair
Yet in her stare

It was clear she could see the secrets
You thought you hid well,
What you tried to quell.
But she could tell,
Sense the smallest cell
Of what befell you,
Your brokenness.

Now she is a woman, confident and brave.
She has found her voice,
Healed from what she forgave,
Free to make her choices
Heard
Her words,
Some soft, some loud, none weak,
Unafraid to speak.
Her words heal,
Feel real enough
To reach the doubting and dispossessed.
They listen to her story,
Leave purgatory,
And give the glory
That is mandatory
To One categorically able to fix
Their brokenness.

Here in My Words

I have been mistaken for cold,
A stone lacking emotion,
A little too controlled,
But my depth is an ocean you could drown in.
Read me and tell me if ice fills my soul.

For here in my words,
Ink poured over pages,
My flesh is exposed,
Naked and vulnerable.
Here in my words,
Outside of armoured cages,
Bare skin uncovered,
Soft and penetrable.

It is here in printed script
I let myself be free,
Untethered, uninhibited,
Unashamed, undone,
Perhaps a bit unhinged to some.
Here in my words,
I let myself be me.

Just Friends

You say let's just be friends.
I say, in this death of romance,
Forever has a chance.
I'll show you all of me,
And you'll reveal all of you,
Only what's true,
No pretence or hesitation,
Just the revelation
That your heart is still safe in my hands.
Our connection sure and secure
As we ever were.

So let romance die, let it burn.
In the fire of friendship, we'll learn.
Nothing can compare, be so intimate,
As souls laid bare, not counterfeit.
No stress trying to impress,
Only living in the truth we profess.
Not lost in a sweet fantasy,
But found in a sweeter reality.
This is what it means
To be "just friends" with me.

Read

I read you like a novel
I couldn't put down.
Enchanted by every word,
I got lost in your story.

For the Last Time

I'm lying in bed,
Struggling to rise,
Reciting speeches in my head.
This is the day I say good-bye to you.
For the last time.
I will confess every part,
Chest splayed open wide,
Displaying my beating heart,
Bleeding heart inside.

He told me I was broken.
He said I couldn't love.
I believed every word.
I believed I wasn't enough.
You made me feel safe enough,
You proved him false,
To fall into your arms,
To let down my walls.

Maybe that's why we met,
So for in that time and place,
I would feel safe enough to let
Someone into my carefully guarded space.
You gave me a glimpse of what it could be.
How beautiful it felt
To love so freely.
But now loving you is hurting me.

I've been holding on.
Can't imagine letting go.
I know that it's wrong.
I need to move on. So...
Like a Band-Aid.
I'll tear you off
Stop picking at this self-inflicted wound.
So the bleeding will stop.

I don't want to become
The broken person I feared to be,
With a heart of stone,
Because you aren't loving me.
This is going to hurt like hell,
Like severing a limb.
But to break free from this spell,
I'll need to cut you out to heal.

I'm sure that I'll cry
As I pour out my heart.
It'll come as no surprise,
You've already read every part.
I'll tell you I love you.
What a gift it has been!
I'll sincerely thank you, too,
Then say good-bye to you again
For the last time.

Try Again

To the degree you allow yourself to love,
To the same degree you risk feeling pain.
But even if you love and lose,
Believe it is worth it to try again.

About the Author

Sharla Fanous was born in Methuen, Massachusetts and she spent most of her young life bouncing around the north-eastern towns north of Boston. Like a true New Englander, she loves fall, football, and Frost poems. She earned a Bachelor's degree in Psychology from Clearwater Christian College and a Master's in Business Leadership and Management from Liberty University.

She moved to Ottawa, ON, Canada in 2007, where she resides with her three children and two cats, T'Challa and Ellie. She can be found binge watching HGTV, experimenting with a new recipe, or chasing around her three rambunctious (but adorable) kids. Jesus and coffee get her through these busy days (and six months of winter!). On rare occasions, she escapes her madhouse to seek the quiet of a local bookstore or engage in deep conversation with a friend.

Sharla is also the author of *Where I Belong: My Journey from Little Girl Lost to Found.*

www.ingramcontent.com/pod-product-compliance
Lightning Source LLC
LaVergne TN
LVHW040905150826
845672LV00007B/1899

* 9 7 8 1 7 7 7 9 1 8 7 4 3 *